THE FORTIES

First published 1985 © International Music Publications
Exclusive Distributors: International Music Publications, Southend Road, Woodford Green, Essex IG8 8HN, England
215-2-272, Order ref: 09908, ISBN 0.86359.244.9
Photocopying of this copyright material is illegal.
Cover design by Howard Brown/Peter Wood. Photography by Peter Wood

ALMOST LIKE BEING IN LOVE

Words by ALAN JAY LERNER
Music by FREDERICK LOEWE

AS TIME GOES BY

Words and Music
by HERMAN HUPFIELD

5

REFRAIN

Moon-light and love songs nev-er out of date, Hearts full of pas-sion, jeal-ous-y and hate;

mf–f poco a poco cresc:

Wo-man needs man and man must have his mate, That no one can de-ny. It's

poco rit.

p–mf

a tempo

still the same old sto-ry, a fight for love and glo-ry, A case of do or die! The

world will al-ways wel-come lov-ers, as time goes by. You by.

f   *mf*   *f*

BEWITCHED

Words by LORENZ HART
Music by RICHARD RODGERS

Moderato

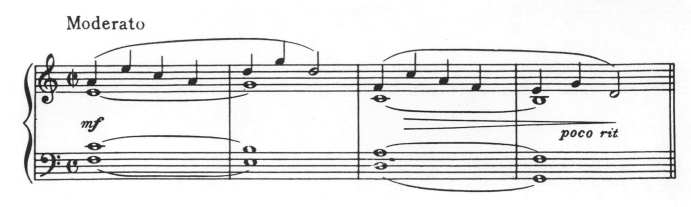

VERSE
(not fast)

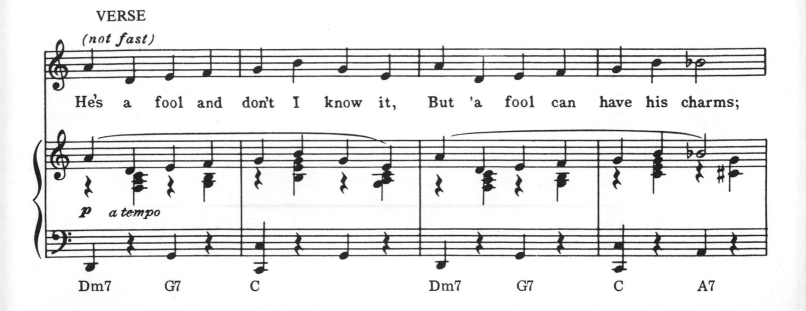

He's a fool and don't I know it, But 'a fool can have his charms;

Dm7   G7   C   Dm7   G7   C   A7

I'm in love and don't I show it, Like a babe in arms.

Dm7   G7   C   Dm7   G7   C

BLUEBERRY HILL

Words and Music by AL LEWIS,
LARRY STOCK and VINCENT ROSE

REFRAIN

DANCE BALLERINA DANCE

Words by BOB RUSSELL
Music by CARL SIGMAN

16

COMING HOME

Words and Music
by BILLY REID

Moderato

Cm6   D7   B♭m6   C7   Fmaj7   Dm7   Gm7   C7

VERSE

Here am I, and there you are, dear, Miles and miles a-part— But 'ab-sence makes the

Cm6   D7   B♭m6   C7   Fmaj7   Dm   Gm7   C7   F

heart grow fond-er'_____ Yet you know for-ev-er you've been

Gm7   F   Gm7   C   Cm6   D7   B♭m6   C7

al-ways in my heart— And we won't have to wait much long-er._____

A7   Dm   G7   C7

REFRAIN

EV'RY TIME WE SAY GOODBYE

Words and Music
by COLE PORTER

22

A GAL IN CALICO

Words by LEO ROBIN
Music by ARTHUR SCHWARTZ

HOW ARE THINGS IN GLOCCA MORRA?

Words by E Y HARBURG
Music by BURTON LANE

HOW HIGH THE MOON

Words by NANCY HAMILTON
Music by MORGAN LEWIS

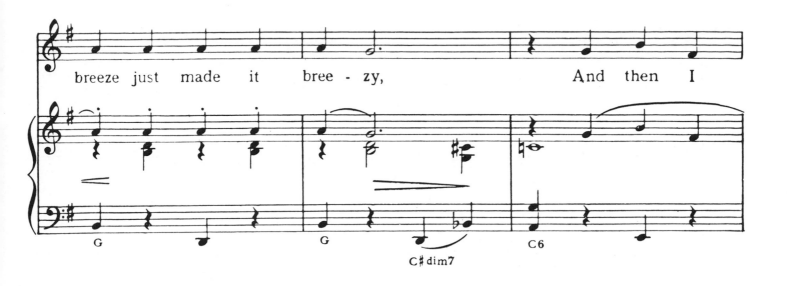

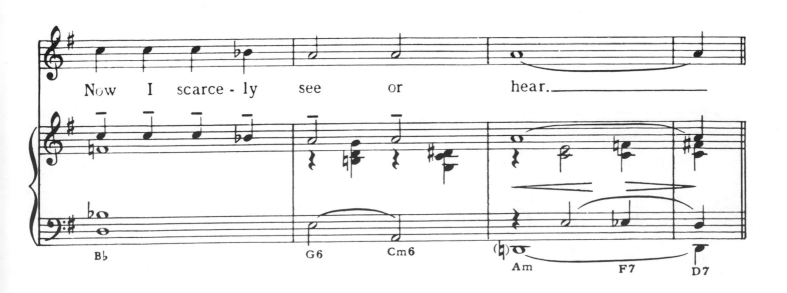

REFRAIN (Slowly, with expression)

Some-where there's mu - sic,___ How faint the tune!___

Some-where there's hea - ven,___ How high the moon!___ There is no

moon a - bove When love is far_ a -way, too,___ Till it comes

true___ That you love me as I love you. Some-where there's

IN THE MOOD

Words by JOE GARLAND
Music by ANDY RAZAF

INTERLUDE

I'LL BE SEEING YOU

Words by IRVING KAHAL
Music by SAMMY FAIN

THE MORE I SEE YOU

Words by MACK GORDON
Music by HARRY WARREN

SEE P. 42 FOR
INTRODUCTION AND VERSE

REFRAIN

The more I see you,___ The more I want you.___ Somehow this

Fm7 Ebdim Eb Bb7 Eb Ebmaj7 Fm7 Bb7 Fm7 Ebdim

feel - ing___ just grows and grows.___ With ev-'ry sigh I be-

Eb Bb7 Eb Bbdim Fm7 Bb7 Fm7 Bb7 Ebm Bb

-come more mad a-bout you,___ more lost with-out you___ And so it

Dbm Gb7 Cb Abm7 Bb7aug Ebm F9

INTRODUCTON AND VERSE

I'LL CLOSE MY EYES

Words and Music
by BILLY REID

REFRAIN

IT MIGHT AS WELL BE SPRING

Words by OSCAR HAMMERSTEIN II
Music by RICHARD RODGERS

THE LAST TIME I SAW PARIS

Words by OSCAR HAMMERSTEIN II
Music by JEROME KERN

Moderato

VERSE

Rhythmically, not too slowly
(in the manner of a simple narrative)

1. A la-dy known as Par-is, Ro-man-tic and charm-ing, Has
2. (I'll) think of hap-py ho-urs, And peo-ple who shared them: Old

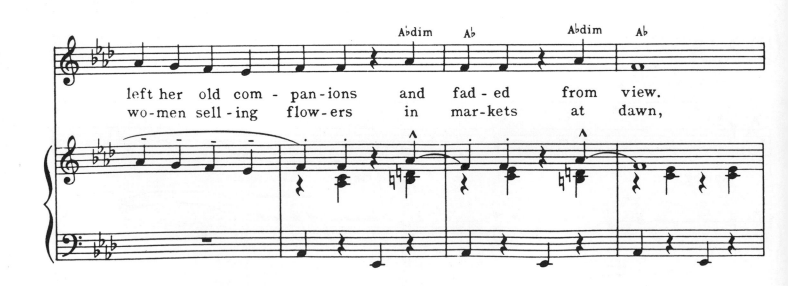

left her old com-pan-ions and fad-ed from view.
wo-men sell-ing flow-ers in mar-kets at dawn,

Lone - ly men with lone - ly eyes are seek-ing her in vain, Her
Chil - dren who ap - plaud-ed Punch and Ju - dy in the park, And

streets are where they were, but there's no sign of her She has left the Seine.
those who danced at night, and kept their Par-is bright Till the town went dark.

REFRAIN
(simply - with rhythm preserved - not sadly)

The last time I saw Par - is Her heart was warm and

gay, I heard the laugh-ter of her heart in ev - 'ry street ca -

53

MOONLIGHT BECOMES YOU

Words by JOHNNY BURKE
Music by JIMMY VAN HEUSEN

SEE P. 56 FOR
INTRODUCTION AND VERSE

REFRAIN

Molto Moderato con expressione

Moon-light be - comes you, It goes with your hair, You cer-tain-ly know the right thing to wear. _____ Moon-light be - comes you, I'm thrilled at the sight, And I could get so ro -

INTRODUCTION AND VERSE

VERSE

Stand there just a mo - ment, dar - ling, let me catch my breath.

I've nev-er see a pic - ture quite so love — ly.

How did you ev - er learn to look so love — ly?

LET THERE BE LOVE

Words by IAN GRANT
Music by LIONEL RAND

REFRAIN

LILLI MARLENE

Words by TOMMIE CONNOR
Original Words by HANS LEIP
Music by NORBERT SHULTZE

A NIGHTINGALE SANG IN BERKELEY SQUARE

Words by ERIC MASCHWITZ
Music by MANNING SHERWIN

an-gels din - ing at the Ritz, And a night-in-gale sang in *Ber - k'ley Square.
ha-zy, cra - zy night we met, When a night-in-gale sang in Ber - k'ley Square.

Eb Bb7 Eb7 Fm7 Eb Cm Fm Bb7 Eb Cm

I may be right, I may be wrong, but I'm perfect-ly will-ing to swear, That
This heart of mine, beat loud and fast, like a mer-ry-go-round in a fair, For

Fm Bb13 Eb Cm Gm Eb Ab G7 Cm Abm6
Bb7+

when you turn'd and smil'd at me, A night-in-gale sang in Ber - k'ley Square.
we were danc - ing cheek to cheek, And a night-in-gale sang in Ber - k'ley Square.

Eb Bb7 Eb Fm7 Eb Cm Fm Bb Eb Cm

The moon that ling-ered ov - er Lon-don Town, poor puzz-led moon, he
When dawn came steal-ing up, all gold and blue, to in - ter - rupt our

Cm6 D7 G Am7 D13 Bm7 Bbo

*Pronounced **Bar** - klee

THE GIPSY

Words and Music
by BILLY REID

Slowly

VERSE

I sit a-lone and dream dear, dream of you night and day, Once you were here_ be-side me, now you are far_ a-way. I've had my for-tune told me, can I be-lieve it's true? Soon we shall be_ to-geth-er, liv-ing our life_ a-new.

66

REFRAIN

TIME AFTER TIME

Words by SAMMY CAHN
Music by JULE STYNE

SEE P. 70 FOR
INTRODUCTION AND VERSE

REFRAIN

Time af - ter time I tell my - self that I'm So

luck-y to be lov - ing you, _____ So luck - y to

be the one you run to see In the eve-ning when the day is

69

INTRODUCTON AND VERSE

LONG AGO (AND FAR AWAY)

Words by IRA GERSHWIN
Music by JEROME KERN

PAPER DOLL

Words and Music
by JOHNNY S BLACK

gone a-way and left me just like all dolls do. I'll tell you boys it's tough to be a

G7   *G*   *G7*   *C7*   *F*   *D7*   *Gm7*   *C7*

-lone   and it's tough to have a doll that's not your own.

F   *F*   *Gm6*   *A7*   *Dm*

I'm thru with all of them, I'll nev-er fall a-gain, 'Cause this is what I'll do.____

C   *Cdim*   *G7*   *C*   *Gm*   *A7*   *D7*   *G7*   *C7*   *Cdim C7*

REFRAIN
Slowly

I'm goin' to buy a PA-PER DOLL that I can call my own, A doll that oth-er fel-lows can-not steal, And then the

F   *F7*   *D7*   *G7*   *C7*   *C+*   *F*

mp-f

76

MY FOOLISH HEART

Words by NED WASHINGTON
Music by VICTOR YOUNG

The night ___ is like a love-ly tune, Be - ware ___ my fool-ish heart! How

B♭   Gm   Cm7   A°

white ___ the ev - er con-stant moon, Take care, ___ my fool-ish heart! There's a

B♭7♮   Gm   Cm7   F7

line be-tween love and fas-ci - na - tion That's hard to see on an eve-ning such as this, For they

B♭   B♭7   B♭+7   E♭   Am7-5   D7-9

both give the ve - ry same sen - sa - tion When you're lost in the mag-ic of a kiss. {His {Her

Gm   D+   Gm7   C9   F7♮   F6   F7   F+9

A LOVELY WAY TO SPEND AN EVENING

Words by HAROLD ADAMSON
Music by JIMMY McHUGH

MAYBE IT'S BECAUSE I'M A LONDONER

Words and Music
by HUBERT GREGG

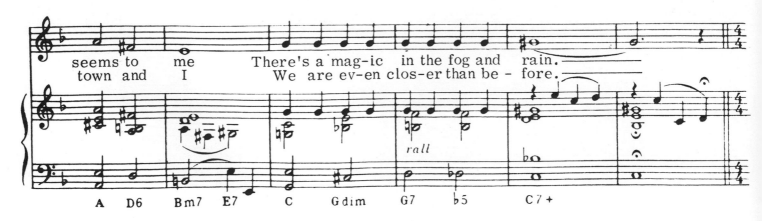

REFRAIN **Slowly** (*with feeling*)

THE NEARNESS OF YOU

Words by NED WASHINGTON
Music by HOAGY CARMICHAEL

87

NOW IS THE HOUR

Words by MAEWA KAIHA
Music by CLEMENT SCOT

THE STARS WILL REMEMBER

Words and Music by
DON PELOSI
and LEO TOWERS

91

TENDERLY

Words by JACK LAWRENCE
Music by WALTER GROSS

Valse moderato

The eve-ning breeze ca-ressed the trees TEN-DER - LY;_____ The tremb-ling

trees em-braced the breeze TEN-DER - LY. _____ Then you and

I came wand-er - ing by And lost in a sigh were

THAT LOVELY WEEKEND

Words and Music by
MOIRA and TED HEATH

WHEN YOU WISH UPON A STAR

Words by NED WASHINGTO
Music by LEIGH HARLIN

WHISPERING GRASS

Words by FRED FISHER
Music by DORIS FISHER

THE WHITE CLIFFS OF DOVER

Words by NAT BURTON
Music by WALTER KENT

101

YOU'LL NEVER KNOW

Words by MACK GORDON
Music by HARRY WARREN

ZIP-A-DEE-DOO-DAH

Words by RAY GILBERT
Music by ALLIE WRUBEL

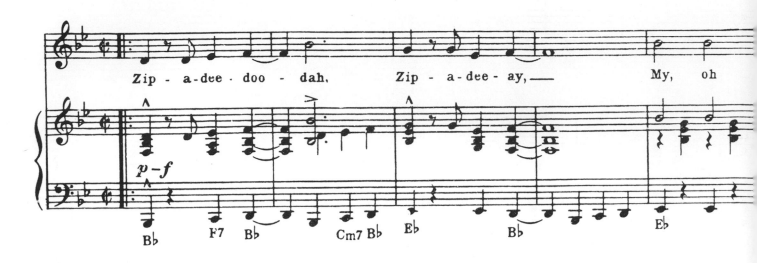

SEE P. 106 FOR
INTRODUCTION AND VERSE

VERSE
Moderately fast

Zip - a-dee - doo - dah, Zip - a-dee - ay,___ My, oh

my,___ what a won - der - ful day!___ Plen - ty of sun-

- shine, head - in' my way,___ Zip - a-dee - doo - dah,

INTRODUCTON AND VERSE

Moderately fast

B♭ VERSE

This is just the kind of day that

you dream a - bout, ___ When you o - pen

up your mouth a song pops out.

YOURS

Words by JACK SHERR
Music by GONZALO ROIG

YOU'VE DONE SOMETHING TO MY HEART

Words by FRANK EYTON and IAN GRANT
Music by NOEL GAY

111

YOU'D BE SO NICE TO COME HOME TO

Words and Music
by COLE PORTER

dar-ling, this is the rea-son Why you've got to be...... mine.

REFRAIN *(Rather slow with feeling)*

You'd be so nice......... to come home to, You'd be

so nice......... by the fire; .... While the breeze on

high......... sang a lul - la - by,......... You'd be all that I could de-

Printed in Great Britain by Hobbs the Printers of Southampton 6/88